Twenty Ways of Looking

poems by

Miriam Weinstein

Finishing Line Press
Georgetown, Kentucky

Twenty Ways of Looking

ACKNOWLEDGMENTS

Deepest gratitude to Jude Nutter for her guidance and insight as my mentor during the
Foreword apprenticeship program in poetry (Loft Literary Center) and for invaluable
support. Hugs and thanks to fellow program members for taking this journey with me;
for thorough critiques along the way, and to Thomas R. Smith for thoughtful comments
and encouragement. Sincere appreciation to Margaret Hasse for nurturing the poet
within me and for her continued counsel. Bravo to members of the Ginger poetry group.
And, especially, to Frances Weinstein for her unwavering love.

To the publications where the following poems first appeared:

Home is a complete sentence, "The Heart of All That Is: Reflections on Home,"
Holy Cow! Press
Memory (take two), "The Quotable"
Best friends and We called them bums, "Word Soup"
God or Renoir at the easel, "Snow Jewel"
On looking, "Evening Street Review"

my heartfelt thanks.

Publisher: Leah Maines

Editor: Christen Kincaid

Cover Art: Miriam Weinstein

Author Photo: Julie Johnson

Cover Design: Elizabeth Maines

Table of Contents

IN MEMORY
of Laurence A. Weinstein
for lighting my path

Before dawn

The hour before dawn lingers
without demands, lingers
without appeals
for attention—
uncluttered
and silent
like an empty
closet
with the door ajar.

Messengers

Any color, any kind—you
who spend your lives on land, you who swim
or soar visit me during days, escort me
through my dreams.

Welcome, birds—one exception:
the European starling with its aggressive, invader
ways. A flock already too many, the throngs
far too much.

Comical, boisterous, and blessed
with a purplish hue, I greet you, common grackle,
arriving in the spring, and your southern boat-tailed
brother is as handsome as can be.

You, blue jay, not a docile, gentle bone, I witnessed
you from my window; your luminous feathers flash
and in a moment's time a fledgling finch lay
lifeless on the ground. Somehow,

I forgive you, Jay, for doing what you do.
Loon, chickadee, warbler, and swan. You, owl,
avian of the night, visit my page and, to places
yet unknown, take my words.

Degrees of separation

It is raining on the tin roof of the orphanage
and on the children in front of the buildings.

They chase each other and jump over puddles
forming on the concrete relic of a driveway.

Packed dirt, loose gravel, and broken slabs.
A small group of children, maybe seven

or eight, are playing hide and seck, but really,
there is no place to hide. Not behind

the motorcycle or the neglected sapling
that has somehow pushed its way up

through a crack in the concrete.
The rain adds to the game

as the puddles grow. The boys' black hair,
heavy with rain, is slicked against their heads;

the girls' dresses cling to their bodies.
There is a rope running between two buildings,

and hanging on it are stained cotton diapers,
underwear, shirts, pants and dresses limp

with rain. Looking at the clothing,
you remember the doll you played with

when you were the size of these children.
A Mary Jane doll that could stand

all by itself if its arms were stretched out
just so. She had freckles across her nose,

and curly blond hair that fell to her shoulders.
More than eight thousand miles away and three

decades ago, it is raining in your backyard.
Just a sprinkle, really. You watch your mother

run outside with a hamper and quickly
scoop flowered sheets and towels

from the clothesline, then run back inside
minutes before rain begins to pelt

the concrete driveway. Everyday you changed
the outfit of your toddler-size doll. Doll clothes

the size of some of the dresses pinned to the rope
strung between buildings of an orphanage.

When you set your doll down to sleep her eyes
closed, and in the morning when you woke her up,

her sky-blue eyes opened to the new day.

No matter how it happened

we share this conundrum:
serpents crawling on their bellies,
humans consumed with shame
and the quest for knowledge;
no escape
from the pain of living;
from our cravings
to touch another person,
to connect,
through the satisfaction
of yearnings sprung up
from love-lust or from the weight
of a hand resting on a shoulder,
from the realization
that when words were spoken,
their meaning was heard
and understood.
Brief moments of abandon
when the self is forgotten;
forgotten long enough to touch
another self
somewhere across the abyss.

There are things I won't write in ink: 1

Details about my father's life wind down columns
of an obituary pulled from an old box. An attempt
to capture his life falls flat in print. Fifteen years.
Dead. This, the first time I've set the word

on paper. A poet who cannot trust words. I circle
his legs, around and between like a cat. Wool
scratching my cheek. Arms reaching
for his knee, his arm reaching

to remove loose change from a pocket, reaching
to loosen his tie, reaching to lift me to his chest.

Sometimes, in the gentle morning rain, I hear
his laughter. Other times, a breeze carries
Old Spice aftershave. Once, sun and shadow
touched at dusk, and I saw

the corner of his lip curve to smile. I cannot trust
words. Ice melts in an arc on pavement.

We called them bums

when I was young, the misfits
scattered around town. Caught,
occasionally, sleeping
during the day
on a park bench,
spotted slipping
at dusk into the forest-like
swath of land brushing
the railroad tracks, emerging
at daybreak to pick through trash,
scavenge in the alleys, appear
out of nowhere and ask: *loose change?*

Today, the hopeless and the homeless
are a regular sight at street corners, store fronts,
and freeway exits. They stand silently, hold
cardboard signs with penciled appeals
and *God Bless* signatures.

This morning the thermometer registers
minus three degrees. Stopped
at a traffic light, I look
at a man standing on a strip
of trampled snow
four feet from me.
Middle-aged, balding
and bare handed,
clutching a sign written
in a child-like scrawl: *Hungry—Homeless—
Anything Helps.* His eyes meet mine.

I reach for my bag and hope the light will quickly
turn green. Extending my arm, I offer a few bills.
His *thank you ma'am* almost lost between
the rumble of idling engines.

Things I thought about this summer

In the State of Nevada prostitution is legal,
and love between homosexuals, a sin.

The Olympic games, a pantheon of skill and power,
is sponsored by *Coca-cola.* Its one-billionth gallon flowed

into a curved bottle during World War II, and now it boasts:
125 years of sharing happiness.

A man who believed a Zionist conspiracy was taking over
the world entered a Sikh temple in Wisconsin,

gunned down six worshippers, then put a bullet
through his White Supremacist head.

When I die, I'd like to be alone on a secluded beach.
A wake of vultures will have what they want

and the rest washed by waves.

As soon as I feel certain of anything, it gives way
under my weight.

Twenty ways of looking at my life

1. I was born on an isthmus between two lakes and learned to swim like a seal.

2. Abundance swam through my childhood.

3. Growing in a world where anything was possible, my parents inspired dreams of abundance.

4. Grandparents, Great-aunties, and Uncles pinched my cheeks wistfully smiling, muttering to each other in a language I did not understand.

5. Yiddish cadences dotted the tones of the English they spoke and laced the language I learned at home.

6. In grade school I learned not to use these words.

7. My mother's words—*Clean your plate*—were followed by a common refrain: *Think of the children starving in China.*

8. I looked at the mashed potatoes and slivers of brisket scattered along the rim of my plate. I saw Chinese children with caps of straight black hair.

9. I settled under oaks that reached towards heaven and I dug. I dug and dug and dug in moist black dirt. I dug through vines and roots in my pursuit—China—on the other side of the world.

10. Television news brought stark images of China and Russia into the homes of middle America.

11. Black and white TV. Black and white photographs. Black and White. Good or Bad. Freedom or Communism.

12. The Bomb. The Arms Race. The Space Race. Communism in Cuba. Adults whispering in solemn tones as I hovered, shaking, in the hallway. Russians arming the island with weapons. Weapons pointing directly at my bedroom window.

13. The movies—my window to the world—for one dollar my friends and I spent summer days in an air-conditioned movie theatre watching the same movie playing again and again.

14. Again and again. And my days spun around

15. and around. And, it's not black or white. There are many shades,

16. shades of grey. I could have been born eighteen years earlier in a ghetto in Poland, a *shtetl* in Russia, a crowded one room apartment in a nameless Romanian town. Unlikely, yes. Impossible—no.

17. I would be another clump of grey ashes swept from a Nazi incinerator. Many heroes became clumps of ashes.

18. Me. I am not a hero. I am anxious—sometimes timid and weak.

19. What then would be the possibility of me? Of me writing this poem.

20. Such happenstance in a world of endless possibilities.

Does writing poetry bring immortal life

or do poems have a life of their own?
After I am dead, if someone reads
my poem will a little kernel of me come back
to life? Or is it enough that I write and someone,
perhaps, may come across my poems
someday. A reader opens an old anthology
where a poem of mine appears and a piece
wedges in her heart. Is my poem then complete
and alive? What about me and my poems,
our life together? What about me
reading a poem I forgot I wrote? Something
stirs. Does that count or are poems truly
unfinished until discovered by another person?

I pause, distracted. Wind blows through bushes,
bluebirds color bowers. I could watch this for hours.

Later, in the *sukkah*, through thin branches and corn stalks
that shelter me, the harvest moon decorates night,
wind snaps against canvas walls, and I try
to count all the stars in the sky.
But I surrender, and sleep.

Sukkah: A temporary hut built for the harvest festival of Sukkot as a reminder of the fragile dwellings Jews lived in for forty years after the Exodus from Egypt. It is topped with branches so the sky is visible.

God or Renoir at the easel

A hallucination of hips floats above the meadow
for hours. One stroke from a grey brush
obliterates a masterpiece.

Here—for a moment

Haunted by images of atomic warfare, dark clouds hovered like helicopters
in my imagination as I ran, ran with a pack of friends across

clipped lawns playing hide-and-seek. Late afternoons, and I followed
my darkening shadow home where arms waited to enfold me.

Hands folded politely in the '50s formed into fists in the '60s, protests
burned along the streets of America, boys broken

or burned in Vietnam and for the first time we witnessed war
while sitting on living room couches,

witnessed bodies lifted from war zones, piled on gurneys, flown home.
The dead—a number at the end of the newscast.

Leaving my childhood home, I found temporary dwellings
dotting the map of North America, I studied

the art of evasion, and learned to avoid the terror beating
in my heart by studying the steady beat of wings

by the shore of Lake Harriet, heartened
to see the fanned formation of geese flying overhead.

Hugging the Baltic Sea—Estonia, Latvia, Lithuania. Fanning out to touch
Russia—Belarus, Ukraine, Kazakhstan. One after the other: Moldova,

Georgia, Armenia, Azerbaijan. The Cold War ended as new countries
formed along river beds and hillsides, one after the other,

Uzbekistan and Turkmenistan. New boundary lines
embraced farm land and forest.

Now, I use the lines of poetry. I write about lines,
and their unlikely intersections. Regardless,

the sun rises at dawn and sets at dusk. Regardless
of what happens between those moments.

Here—for a moment.

Moments—more than minutes, or hours, more than days
or weeks or months—matter. Moments turn into years as the earth

spins around. Mother earth. Weighed down

by bones, I yearn for the hollow bones of a bird
so that, like a pelican, I could follow rivers to a lake forming

in the Australian desert. I could grow fat on fish flourishing there.
More likely, I will grow old here in the land of 10,000 lakes

where loons have always flourished, their tremolos
cutting the darkness.

Mementos

Found every few years during a cleaning binge of the basement,
in boxes, and bins, and old wooden crates: mementos once full
of meaning—covered now with dust—keep company

with other mementos, cobwebs for companions. Under high school
reports, teenage love letters, an autograph book with silly rhymes
and fourth grade signatures, I discover a letter box

with an embossed pattern on the lid and my name in block letters.
Inside, a faded pink ribbon rests on top of my birth announcement
and the ledger where Mom's tidy script tracked daily feedings.

Somewhere on a shelf, somewhere nearby inside a plastic bin
is a journal with details about my daughter's first years,
a growth chart, and a lock of her curly, black hair.

Mementos. I watch my daughter, a mother herself now,
write in a spiral notebook about her baby: feeding times,
amounts, his hours of sleep. Where, when full,

will she keep this notebook? I hesitate to return my *baby box*
to where it was found. Where does it belong? Where,
in the end, do any of these mementos belong?

I place my box in soil moist and welcoming; I bury it as if
it were a threadbare bible. The box rests under a rosebush
named *Aloha*. Climbing on a trellis every summer

Aloha reaches for the sun. Dissolving in dirt will
mementos fertilize my garden?

On looking

Have you ever looked at someone, someone
who you've known for years and in that moment

seen a face you've never seen before?
The deep blue-green eyes are there

and the dimple on the chin unchanged, but startled
you realize you've never really seen this person

even though you've looked at her more times
than you can remember.

Is it the tilt of her head, the way sunlight slants
across her face, the shadow cast as someone

moves past, the growing noise at the party
that causes you to move closer

as you converse? She could be a neighbor
you visit often, a friend you meet weekly for lunch,

a buddy in your book group that gathers the first
Sunday evening, every month.

How many people have you really seen?
How many people see you, really?

All the time you take setting your image just so.
Clothing, cosmetics, and jewelry chosen to provide

clues about who you are. What are you looking for
when you scan your face? Would you recognize it,

if you saw it? Maybe all these years you've looked
past the one who stands before you.

Mame-loshin (mother tongue)
A Yiddish proverb: The whole world
is a dream and death the interpreter.

There once was a family—a tender mother, a proud
father, a son and a daughter. Their home was filled, often,
with more uncles and aunts and cousins
than the children could count. Death's hand
rarely touched this family.
Once or twice in a crowded kitchen the girl
heard muffled sobs as she wove between long legs.
Cigarette smoke and the aroma of freshly
baked strudel in the air. Thinking back,

the girl remembers a great-aunt,
her wide bosom, her chocolate-brown eyes,
the guttural sounds of her *mame-loshin*,
and *taiglech* with drops of dried honey hanging
from balls of sweet dough. The girl doesn't remember
when the table was first empty of this treat.

One morning the girl awoke and found she was a young woman.
Her head and heart filled with urges she could not name.
Traveling far from her family, she studied foreign
languages, theatre, and photography. When she went out
at night she wore different masks. Scholar,
actress, artist. Precariously

perched across the country, she learned of deaths during Sunday
talks with her parents. *Der Alter Mishpocha*, straddlers of two worlds,
followed each other to the grave—*Mame-loshin* teetered
on the edge. The decline of her aunt shaded half a decade,
the aunt who attempted to teach her to sew, the aunt
who invited her to work sweet dough to perfection.

Once
she fashioned a family of her own, nourished her children
as best she could. Days of their childhood spread over seasons
she relished and remembers; the compassion of her parents
enriched her tent of one mother, two daughters. Then,
it was her own father. And time stopped.

The family hovered around his hospital bed, later
swayed, shoulders pressed together
during seven days of *shiva*.

Then time galloped off—the woman hanging on, no reins
for guidance—

now, a grandmother, the woman finds herself aware of only a few
mame-loshin phrases to call her own, yet remembers lullabies
in a language she sings to her grandchildren. And

deaths pile up like pebbles on the beach
where she had once played as a child.

Best friends

I

Whose idea was it to open that new box of felt-tip
Magic Markers? I yanked out the red one, Patty pulled
at the blue one, then, all the markers slid
onto the floor of the Ladies Room. In a frenzy

of fun we decorated the toilet stalls: *Patty loves Joey*
with a big red heart around the letters and an arrow
piercing it. *True Love* with an identical design.
Oblivious to the commotion we caused,

who heard the door fly open, who saw the uniformed
clerk enter? Marched up stairs to the manager, told:
Actions have consequences. Mom, so ashamed,
I never expected such behavior from you.

It was clear Patty was the problem.
Actions have consequences buzzed like an angry
bee all night long. Saturday morning at Woolworth's,
cleaning supplies in hand paid for with next week's

allowance money, we scrubbed the entire
bathroom, all signs of our pre-teen love

gone.

II

Patty went on to meet trouble: With boys,
with alcohol, with her work as a stripper

in a bar across town. Patty went on to forget
actions have consequences. Plagued,

with an untethered temper, she turned friends
and fellow workers to foes. Plagued

with untreated mental illness, she fueled fires
in her family. When Patty took unpaid

leave to help her terminally ill mother,
she was terminated. Patty flared, raged

out of control and plunged. *Fifty dollars left,*
she told me last week. Eligible for disability,

she never applied. Eligible for social security,
she's clueless what to do. *Food stamps*

won't pay for toilet paper.

Awake before dawn   I see Patty
homeless and on the street—homeless and with shards

of glass around her feet.

There are things I won't write in ink: 2

I thumb through my thesaurus longing for insight.
I hear the song of the meadowlark encouraging me
to trust words. *There are things I won't write*

in ink. Try pencil, she sings. Graphite on paper.

Like a clumsy child, a thick yellow pencil in hand,
I form block letters. Capitals first, I stiffly shape
the pointed tops of A's, the rounded hats of B's.

Half moon C's and D's rise on paper alone without
meaning. Slowly, I place one letter next to another
in different configurations. Slowly I create words

with meaning, words I can learn to trust.

Memory (take two)

Aunt Essie is sure she and my uncle drove Sally and me
to the Beatles concert in Milwaukee, 1964.
Mom is sure she and Dad drove us, says we visited
my aunt, uncle, and cousins before the concert. Then
Dad did the driving. Mom remembers watching
me get swallowed by the crowd, wondering
if I still had Sally's hand. She'd insisted
we hold hands in the crowd. Bedlam.
That's what is was. The Beatles in America.
Crowds swelling outside concert halls,
moving like a single body.

My cousin says:
Your parents didn't even come to Milwaukee.
You and Sally rode the Badger Bus from Madison.
I was so jealous I couldn't go to the concert.
I still have the button you bought me.

Memory is funny though, she admits.
I wouldn't bet on it. That winding road behind us
under constant reconstruction.

Over and over again

We play Hide and Seek, scattering like wild colts
across unfenced yards, one child left
on the grassy triangle counting—*three, four*—
leaping over boxwood hedges, vaulting

over flower beds. *Nineteen, twenty . . . ready or not.*
Here I come. The door of Mr. Sweet's old shed flaps
in the wind as he sweeps the driveway. I enter and duck
behind the lawn mower which is still warm. Friends

dart by, boys and girls squeal when found and bolt
past the shed to begin the game again. I hug my legs
and fall asleep. When I wake it's dark. Pitch black.
I scramble to my knees, knock against flower

pots as I search for the door—locked while I slept—
I bang and bang, louder and louder. Finally,
my father's voice comes closer and closer
calling my name.

English Breakfast tea and me

Born to first generation Americans and proud
consumers of coffee, the aroma of brewing beans

percolated through my childhood filling the air
with the fragrance of the American dream. Freedom.

Hard work. Prosperity. Tea, a drink
from the old country, appeared occasionally.

A bag of *Lipton's* quickly dunked in warm water.
Tepid, tan, and tasteless. Somehow the art

of brewing tea seeped into me. Fleeing pogroms
in Eastern Europe, did a link of my family chain

take haven in towns dotting the shores of an island
in the Atlantic? Yearning for a new life,

did they pack away their samovars and embrace
the British way of preparing tea? I spoon loose

leaves into a pre-warmed *Brown Betty*, bring water
to a rapid boil, fill the teapot, and cover it

with a thick tea-cozy resembling a fur cap
popular among Russian soldiers.

The leaves steep a full five minutes. A soothing
flavor slowly released releases me. Inventing

a past, creating a future: I sip and savor.

Home is a complete sentence

Home.

The almost silent, breathy capital H.
Two solid pillars with a straight bar between them
like a rung on a ladder or a bridge.

Stability in two limbs.

And there you are: Half way up one side, resting.
Will you complete the precarious walk

across what now looks like a very thin balance beam?
Risk slipping and falling into the perfect circular pond

of the neighboring o? If you fall, will someone throw you
another smaller o, a life ring to float on, or a piece of the H
for support while you catch your breath?

Now, on the edge of the o, it's either back over to hang on
the ladder of H for safety, or time to move on.

Look at those two massive mountains of the m ahead of you,
three quarters of the way across the sentence. Home.
The trek along m is worth it.

You know what's on the other side. A swirl in the tail of e
where you can rest. Yet e is fraught with expectations

of embraces; or, at least, half embraces
as the e stands there at the end—not fully closed.
But go on. Slide off

the e and then hop over that period.
Go on.

Begin your own sentence.

Miriam Weinstein first ventured into verse with a poetic rant addressed to President Nixon; it was several decades before she enrolled in a poetry class. Weinstein completed a two year apprenticeship program in poetry at the Loft Literary Center (Minneapolis) in 2013. Her poetry appears in several journals and an anthology by Holy Cow! Press *The Heart of All That Is: Reflections on Home.* Weinstein holds two Master of Education degrees (Adult and Family Life Education) from the University of Minnesota and a Bachelor of Arts degree (Dramatic Arts) from the University of Winnipeg. She has worked in these fields and as a photographer. Her black and white gelatin silver prints have been exhibited in the Midwest. Weinstein lives close to Minnehaha Creek in Minneapolis and enjoys walking along the extensive trails that wind beside its banks. This is her first chapbook.

CPSIA information can be obtained at www.ICGtesting.com
Printed in the USA
LVOW08s0730080716

495308LV00003B/42/P